THE WOMAN OF ENNEAGRAM 7

LOVE, MARRIAGE AND SUCCESS EDITION

FREE GIFT

Get a FREE book on the Enneagram & Female Sexuality! Discover:
Fears & desires
Sexual traits
Sexual compatibility
Tips for a fulfilling sex life
Limited time offer!

The woman of Enneagram 7: Love marriage success edition

Enneagram For Women, Volume 7

Maria Rondon

Published by Maria Rondon, 2024.

While every precaution has been taken in the preparation of this book, the publisher assumes no responsibility for errors or omissions, or for damages resulting from the use of the information contained herein.

THE WOMAN OF ENNEAGRAM 7: LOVE MARRIAGE SUCCESS EDITION

First edition. March 28, 2024.

Copyright © 2024 Maria Rondon.

ISBN: 979-8227442253

Written by Maria Rondon.

<u>OR CLICK HERE</u>[1]

---

1. https://divinemessenger.site/free-gift/

ENNEAGRAM 7 FOR WOMEN.
Copyright © 2024 by Maria Rondon
All rights reserved. Printed in Catalunya, Spain.
No part of this book may be used or reproduced in any manner whatsoever without written permission except in the case of brief quotations embodied in critical articles and reviews. For information address Sans Serif Agency, Girona, Catalunya, Spain.
Want more books at discount:
http://www.divinemessenger.site
Sans Serif Agency is a trademark of Sans Serif Agency.
Library of Congress Cataloging-in-Publication Data:
Rondon, Maria.
Enneagram 7 for women / Maria Rondon. — 1st ed.

CONTENT

Chapter 1: Charting Your Course: The Enneagram and the Thriving Woman

A brief exploration of the Enneagram's history and its unique value for women seeking self-discovery.

Unveiling the power of self-awareness: How understanding your "7ness" empowers you in all areas of life.

Chapter 2: The Enthusiastic Woman: Embracing Your Zest for Life

Unveiling the core motivations, desires, fears, and defining characteristics of the Type 7 woman.

Exploring the two instinctual subtypes (self-preservation and social) and their influence on your personality.

Chapter 3: Building Bridges, Not Walls: The Enneagram and Relationships

Harnessing the Enneagram to understand type differences and cultivate stronger, more fulfilling relationships.

Chapter 4: Cultivating Joyful Connections: Trust and Security in Relationships

Understanding the central role of trust and security in your relationships as a Type 7 woman.

Developing effective communication strategies to strengthen bonds with partners, friends, and family.

Chapter 5: Find Your Flock: Building Supportive Networks

Recognizing the importance of strong friendships and social connections for your well-being.

Practical tips for building and nurturing meaningful relationships with friends and colleagues.

Chapter 6: Igniting Your Spark: Finding Purpose in Career and Vocation

Identifying your unique strengths and passions to discover a fulfilling career path.

Conquering indecision and overcoming fear of failure in the workplace.

Chapter 7: Building Inner Strength: Resilience and Self-Acceptance

Developing resilience to bounce back from challenges and conquer self-criticism.

Practical techniques for managing anxiety and cultivating self-compassion.

Chapter 8: Mind-Body Harmony: Cultivating Wholeness

Exploring the connection between mindful eating and your physical and emotional well-being.

Discovering the role of exercise in stress management and overall health.

Chapter 9: Deepening Your Connection: The Enneagram and Spirituality

Utilizing the Enneagram as a tool to connect with your spiritual core. Exploring various spiritual practices that resonate with the Type 7 woman.

Chapter 10: Unveiling Your Wings: Exploring the Nuances of Your Personality

Delving into the concept of wings (Type 7w5 and Type 7w8) and their influence on your strengths, challenges, and overall personality.

Chapter 11: Growth and Transformation: Integration and Disintegration

Understanding the path of integration towards Type 8 (increased focus and discipline) and disintegration towards Type 1 (perfectionism and negativity) for the Type 7 woman.

Chapter 12: Workbook

Chapter 1:

Charting Your Course: The Enneagram and the Thriving Woman

A Brief Exploration of the Enneagram's History and Its Unique Value for Women Seeking Self-Discovery

Embarking on the journey of self-discovery can often seem like navigating through an intricate maze, filled with twists and turns that challenge our perceptions and beliefs about ourselves. In the quest for personal growth and fulfillment, women across the globe have turned to various tools and methodologies to uncover the layers of their being and harness their true potential. Among these tools, the Enneagram stands out as a beacon of insight, offering a profound framework for understanding the complexities of human personality and behavior. This chapter delves into the rich tapestry of the Enneagram's history and its singular value for women on the path to self-discovery.

The Enneagram's origins, shrouded in the mists of time, are as fascinating as the system itself. Its roots can be traced back to ancient spiritual and philosophical traditions, embodying a confluence of wisdom from diverse cultures. The symbol, a nine-pointed figure, encapsulates the unity and diversity of human nature, serving as a mirror reflecting the multifaceted aspects of the human psyche.

Historically, the Enneagram's journey from an esoteric symbol to a tool for self-understanding and growth is marked by the contributions of various thinkers and mystics. George Gurdjieff and Peter Ouspensky, early proponents of the Enneagram in the 20th century, played pivotal roles in introducing the system to the Western world. Their teachings emphasized the Enneagram's potential for awakening and self-realization, laying the groundwork for its application in personal development.

As the Enneagram's teachings spread, scholars and spiritual teachers like Claudio Naranjo, Oscar Ichazo, and Helen Palmer enriched the system with their insights, exploring the psychological dimensions of the nine personality types. Their work illuminated the intricate dynamics of human behavior, motivations, and fears, offering individuals a roadmap to navigate their inner landscapes.

For women, in particular, the Enneagram holds unique value. In a world where women often navigate complex social, cultural, and personal expectations, the Enneagram serves as a tool for empowerment and self-assertion. By uncovering the underlying motivations and patterns that shape their lives, women can embark on a transformative journey of self-acceptance and growth. The Enneagram provides a language for understanding the self and others, fostering empathy, communication, and deeper connections.

Moreover, the Enneagram's holistic approach to personality and development resonates with the experiences of many women, who seek to balance various roles and identities in their lives. Through the lens of the Enneagram, women can explore the interplay between their inner world and external realities, gaining insights into how they can thrive amidst challenges and transitions.

As women chart their course toward self-discovery and personal fulfillment, the Enneagram offers a compass to guide their journey. It invites them to explore the depths of their being, to embrace their strengths and vulnerabilities, and to live authentically in alignment with their true selves. In the spirit of the ancient traditions from which it emerged, the Enneagram encourages women to embark on a path of self-knowledge and transformation, leading them toward a life of purpose, empowerment, and joy.

In the subsequent sections, we will explore the nuances of the Enneagram types, shedding light on the distinctive journeys of women as they navigate the contours of their personalities. By understanding the intricate web of motivations, fears, and desires that drive their actions, women can unlock the door to a more fulfilled and authentic existence. The Enneagram, with its rich history and profound insights, serves as a trusted ally in the quest for self-discovery and personal growth.

Unveiling the Power of Self-Awareness: How Understanding Your "7ness" Empowers You in All Areas of Life

In the rich tapestry of human personality, the Enneagram Type 7, often known as the Enthusiast, shines brightly with a zest for life and an insatiable curiosity for all that the world has to offer. This chapter is dedicated to women who identify with or are exploring the vibrant energy of Type 7 within the Enneagram system. It is a deep dive into how understanding and embracing your "7ness" can serve as a powerful catalyst for personal empowerment, growth, and fulfillment across all facets of life.

Type 7s are characterized by their optimistic outlook, versatility, and spontaneous spirit. They possess an innate ability to see the world through a lens of endless possibilities, often driven by a desire to experience joy, avoid pain, and keep their options open. However, this same zest for life can sometimes lead to restlessness, overextension, and a tendency to avoid facing deeper, more complex emotions.

The journey of self-awareness for a woman embodying Type 7 begins with recognizing these inherent traits, both the strengths and the challenges. It involves delving into the nuances of her personality, understanding the motivations behind her pursuit of pleasure and variety, and acknowledging the parts of herself that she may prefer to keep in the shadows. This process of self-exploration is not merely an exercise in introspection but a gateway to transformative growth and empowerment.

Empowerment Through Emotional Depth and Acceptance

One of the profound benefits of embracing your "7ness" is the cultivation of emotional depth and acceptance. For Type 7s, the instinctive avoidance of pain or discomfort can be a barrier to experiencing the full spectrum of human emotions. However, by confronting and embracing these feelings, women of this type can unlock a new level of emotional resilience and authenticity. This acceptance does not diminish the natural joy and enthusiasm that define Type 7s but enriches it with a deeper understanding of self and others.

Thriving in Relationships and Connections

Understanding your "7ness" also holds the key to nurturing fulfilling relationships. The natural enthusiasm and energy of Type 7 women can be infectious, drawing others toward them with ease. However, the journey of self-awareness invites these women to explore the quality of their connections, encouraging them to cultivate deeper, more meaningful relationships. By acknowledging their fears of commitment or depth and embracing vulnerability, Type 7 women can experience a newfound intimacy and connection that complements their vibrant social life.

Harnessing Creativity and Vision

Type 7s are natural visionaries, often blessed with a creativity that knows no bounds. Their ability to see possibilities where others see limitations is a unique strength. Self-awareness allows these women to channel their boundless energy and ideas into tangible achievements.

By understanding their tendency to jump from one interest to another, they can learn to harness their focus, bringing their visions to life with determination and purpose.

Cultivating Mindfulness and Presence

Perhaps one of the most transformative aspects of understanding your "7ness" is the journey towards mindfulness and presence. The restless energy of Type 7 can often lead to a scattered focus and a disconnection from the present moment. Self-awareness invites women of this type to slow down, savor the now, and appreciate the beauty in simplicity. This shift not only enhances their personal well-being but also deepens their appreciation for life's journey, moment by moment.

In the landscape of self-discovery, understanding and embracing your Type 7 personality is akin to unlocking a treasure chest of potential. It is about acknowledging the fullness of who you are, with all your complexities, strengths, and vulnerabilities. For women navigating the path of Type 7, this journey of self-awareness is not just about personal growth; it's about empowerment. It's about stepping into your power, embracing your innate resilience and joy, and thriving in every area of life.

As we chart the course for the thriving woman, let us remember that the journey of self-discovery is both deeply personal and universally resonant. The Enneagram, with its ancient roots and modern applications, serves as a compass guiding us toward a deeper understanding of ourselves and our place in the world. For the Type 7 woman, this journey is not just about uncovering the essence of her "7ness" but about embracing it as a source of strength, inspiration, and boundless potential.

Chapter 2:

The Enthusiastic Woman: Embracing Your Zest for Life

Unveiling the Core Motivations, Desires, Fears, and Defining Characteristics of the Type 7 Woman

Within the intricate weave of the Enneagram's wisdom, the Type 7 woman emerges as a figure of joy, exuberance, and a boundless zest for life. This chapter delves into the heart of what it means to navigate the world as a Type 7, exploring the core motivations, desires, fears, and the defining characteristics that shape the journey of the Enthusiastic Woman.

Core Motivations and Desires

At the core of every Type 7 woman lies a profound desire for freedom and happiness. This is not merely a longing for ephemeral joys but a deep-seated drive to experience life in its fullest, most vibrant form. The Type 7 woman is propelled by an innate urge to explore, to discover, and to savor the myriad flavors of existence. She seeks to create a life that is rich with experiences, where variety and novelty serve as the fuel for her ever-burning fire of enthusiasm.

This thirst for experiences is rooted in a fundamental motivation to avoid pain and discomfort. The Type 7 woman, with her optimistic and forward-looking gaze, often focuses on positive possibilities, sometimes to the extent of sidestepping the more challenging aspects of life. Her pursuit of happiness is not just about seeking pleasure but about maintaining a sense of autonomy and inner peace in a world that can often seem limiting and filled with adversity.

Fears and Challenges

The luminous path of the Type 7 woman is not without its shadows. Her fear of being trapped in emotional pain or constrained by circumstances can lead to a pattern of escapism. This fear often manifests as a restlessness, a sense that no matter how much is achieved or experienced, it might never be enough to fully satiate her hunger for life.

Another significant challenge for the Type 7 woman is confronting the depth of her own emotions. In her quest to remain uplifted, she may inadvertently skirt around deeper feelings of sadness, anger, or fear, thereby missing out on the full spectrum of human emotional experience. This avoidance can sometimes hinder her ability to form deep, lasting connections, as true intimacy requires vulnerability and the courage to face life's inevitable sorrows alongside its joys.

Defining Characteristics

The Enthusiastic Woman is a beacon of light and energy. She is defined by her optimism, her creativity, and her ability to see opportunities where others see obstacles. Her mind is a kaleidoscope of ideas, plans, and possibilities, always moving, always dreaming. This agility of thought and passion for exploration make her an inspiring presence, capable of leading others toward a more positive, expansive view of life.

Type 7 women are also characterized by their adaptability and resilience. Their natural inclination to seek out the silver lining, to bounce back from setbacks with renewed vigor, speaks to a profound inner strength. It is this resilience that enables them to navigate life's ups and downs with grace and to use their experiences as stepping stones for growth and self-discovery.

Embracing Your Zest for Life

For the Type 7 woman, understanding and embracing her core motivations, desires, fears, and defining characteristics is a journey of empowerment. It is about recognizing her innate strengths while also confronting the areas where growth is needed. By acknowledging her fears and embracing her depth of emotion, the Type 7 woman can transform her restlessness into a purposeful quest for a fulfilled and balanced life.

This chapter invites Type 7 women to see their zest for life not just as a quest for personal pleasure, but as a gift to be shared with the world. It is an encouragement to harness their enthusiasm, creativity, and resilience in a way that not only enriches their own lives but also inspires those around them. In embracing the full spectrum of their experience, including the shadows and the light, Type 7 women can truly thrive, living as embodiments of joy, freedom, and boundless possibility.

Exploring the Two Instinctual Subtypes (Self-Preservation and Social) and Their Influence on Your Personality

As we journey deeper into the vibrant landscape of the Enneagram, specifically within the realm of Type 7, the enthusiastic woman, we encounter a fascinating dimension that further enriches our understanding of personality: the instinctual subtypes. These subtypes, self-preservation and social, act as nuanced lenses through which we view the world, influencing our behaviors, desires, and fears in profound ways. This exploration reveals how these instinctual energies shape the unique expression of zest for life that defines the Type 7 woman.

The Self-Preservation Subtype: Seeking Security in a World of Plenty

The self-preservation instinct in a Type 7 woman drives her to seek security and comfort, but with a distinctive twist. Unlike other types where self-preservation might manifest as a focus on physical safety and well-being, for the Type 7, this instinct intertwines with their inherent desire for pleasure and variety. The self-preservation Type 7 seeks to create a world where freedom from pain and discomfort is paramount, not just in the physical sense but also in terms of maintaining a positive and stimulating environment.

This subtype is often characterized by a keen ability to find creative solutions to problems, ensuring that their needs are met in ways that align with their desire for an enjoyable and comfortable life. They are adept at navigating the material world in a manner that maximizes their joy and minimizes their exposure to distress. However, this relentless pursuit of comfort can sometimes lead to avoidance behaviors, where the self-preservation Type 7 might ignore deeper issues or challenges, preferring instead to focus on the lighter, more pleasurable aspects of life.

The Social Subtype: The Pursuit of Belonging Through Joy

The social instinct in a Type 7 woman amplifies her natural inclination towards enthusiasm and connection. This subtype seeks to create a sense of belonging and acceptance through shared experiences and joy. The social Type 7 is often the life of the party, using their charm, wit, and vivacity to foster connections and bring people together. They are driven by a desire to be valued and appreciated within their social circles, often going to great lengths to ensure that their contributions are recognized and celebrated.

However, this drive for social belonging can also reveal underlying fears of being left out or deemed unworthy of love and attention. The social Type 7 may find themselves overcommitting to social engagements or projects, fearing that saying no might result in isolation or a loss of status within their community. Their challenge lies in finding balance, learning to cultivate genuine connections that allow for both the expression of their vibrant personality and the acceptance of their vulnerabilities.

Navigating the World with Your Instinctual Subtype

Understanding your instinctual subtype as a Type 7 woman offers invaluable insights into the ways in which you engage with the world around you. Whether driven by the self-preservation instinct, with its focus on comfort and security, or by the social instinct, with its emphasis on connection and recognition, recognizing your subtype can illuminate paths to growth and fulfillment.

For the self-preservation Type 7, growth may involve confronting the deeper issues they have been avoiding, learning that true security comes from facing life's challenges head-on. For the social Type 7, growth might mean cultivating deeper, more authentic relationships, where their worth is recognized beyond their ability to entertain and uplift.

Embracing your subtype is not about limiting yourself to a particular way of being but rather about deepening your understanding of your motivations, fears, and desires. It is a step towards embracing your full self, leveraging your natural zest for life while acknowledging the complex, multifaceted nature of your personality. As you explore the influence of your instinctual subtype, you unlock new dimensions of your identity, paving the way for a life of true enthusiasm, connection, and personal fulfillment.

Chapter 3:

Building Bridges, Not Walls: The Enneagram and Relationships

Harnessing the Enneagram to Understand Type Differences and Cultivate Stronger, More Fulfilling Relationships

In the journey of self-discovery and personal growth, the Enneagram serves as a profound tool not only for understanding oneself but also for deepening our understanding of others. The intricacies of human relationships can often be complex and challenging, yet the wisdom of the Enneagram offers a beacon of light, guiding us towards stronger, more fulfilling connections. This chapter explores how leveraging the Enneagram's insights into personality type differences can be transformative in cultivating relationships that are built on understanding, respect, and mutual growth.

The Power of Understanding Type Differences

At its core, the Enneagram illuminates the diverse lenses through which we view the world, highlighting the distinct motivations, fears, and desires that drive our behaviors. Recognizing these differences is paramount in relationships, as it fosters a deeper empathy and acceptance for the other's unique way of being. When we begin to understand that the root of our partner's, friend's, or colleague's actions often lies in their core Enneagram type, we can move beyond surface-level frustrations to a place of compassionate understanding.

For example, recognizing that a Type 2's actions are driven by a desire to be loved and appreciated can transform our interpretation of their behavior from being overly needy to being seen as expressions of love. Similarly, understanding a Type 5's need for alone time as a necessity for recharging, rather than a rejection, can significantly alleviate feelings of neglect or misunderstanding in relationships.

Bridging the Gap Through Communication

One of the most profound benefits of utilizing the Enneagram in relationships is its ability to enhance communication. By understanding the communication style and needs of each type, we can tailor our interactions in ways that resonate deeply with our loved ones. The Enneagram encourages us to speak the language of the other's heart, whether it requires affirming words of encouragement for a Type 3 striving for success or offering gentle space and understanding to a Type 4 in their moments of emotional depth.

Moreover, the Enneagram can guide us in addressing conflicts and challenges with sensitivity and awareness. It teaches us that our instinctual reactions may not always align with the needs or perceptions of other types. By stepping into the shoes of another's Enneagram type, we gain invaluable insights into the most constructive ways to approach delicate situations, paving the way for resolutions that honor the dignity and perspective of all involved.

Cultivating Growth-Oriented Relationships

Perhaps one of the most transformative aspects of applying the Enneagram in relationships is the potential for mutual growth. The Enneagram does not merely stop at understanding and acceptance; it invites us into a dynamic process of evolving alongside our partners and friends. By being aware of each other's strengths and growth edges, we can support one another in our journeys of personal development.

This mutual growth process is enriched by the Enneagram's pathway for each type, which outlines both healthy and unhealthy expressions of their behaviors and motivations. Couples and friends can explore these paths together, celebrating each other's progress, and gently holding one another accountable to the work of overcoming personal limitations and embracing greater self-awareness and transformation.

The Enneagram as a Relationship Compass

The Enneagram's ancient wisdom offers timeless insights into the human heart and mind, making it an invaluable compass for navigating the complexities of relationships. By harnessing its power to understand type differences, we open the door to more empathetic, communicative, and growth-oriented connections. The journey of building bridges, not walls, is a testament to the transformative potential of the Enneagram in fostering relationships that are not only stronger and more fulfilling but also serve as catalysts for personal and collective evolution.

As we continue to explore the depths of our own types and those of the people around us, let us remember that the essence of the Enneagram is love—love for ourselves, for others, and for the journey of growth that we share. In this light, the Enneagram becomes more than just a tool for understanding; it becomes a pathway to a more connected, compassionate, and vibrant world.

Chapter 4:

Cultivating Joyful Connections: Trust and Security in Relationships

Understanding the Central Role of Trust and Security in Your Relationships as a Type 7 Woman

For the Type 7 woman, embarking on a voyage through life with an undying zest and enthusiasm, the concepts of trust and security hold profound significance in the realm of relationships. This chapter delves into the intricate dynamics of these elements, exploring their essential role in nurturing joyful and enduring connections. For the enthusiastic woman, whose spirit thrives on exploration and adventure, trust and security serve as anchors, providing a foundation upon which meaningful and lasting relationships can be built.

The Essence of Trust for the Type 7 Woman

Trust, in its myriad forms, is a cornerstone of healthy relationships. For the Type 7 woman, trust encompasses more than just fidelity or reliability; it signifies a deeper affirmation of her inherent need for freedom and spontaneity. To trust is to know that her partners and friends appreciate and celebrate her vivacity, without seeking to clip her wings. It means embracing her boundless energy and enthusiasm, while providing a safe space for her to land when she tires from her flights of fancy.

However, cultivating trust poses unique challenges for the Type 7, whose natural inclination to avoid pain and seek pleasure can sometimes manifest as an aversion to vulnerability. True trust requires the courage to be vulnerable, to share not only the highs but also the lows, the fears alongside the dreams. For the Type 7 woman, learning to embrace vulnerability is akin to unlocking a new dimension of her relationships, one where trust deepens through shared experiences of both joy and sorrow.

Security: A Haven for the Adventurous Spirit

Security in relationships, for the Type 7 woman, does not imply restriction or confinement but rather a sense of emotional safety and stability. It is knowing that her need for variety and adventure is not merely tolerated but understood and valued. Security means having a base of operations, a haven of acceptance and love, from which she can launch into the world, assured of a warm welcome upon her return.

This sense of security is crucial in mitigating the Type 7's fear of being trapped or suffocated by commitments. It reassures her that true commitment does not equate to the loss of her essence or freedom. Instead, it represents a mutual journey of growth and discovery, where the bonds of love are strengthened by the willingness to explore the vast terrains of life together.

Cultivating Trust and Security: Practical Insights

For the Type 7 woman, cultivating trust and security begins with self-awareness. Recognizing her tendencies to shy away from discomfort or conflict is the first step towards addressing them. It involves a conscious effort to engage in open, honest communication, expressing needs and desires candidly while also being receptive to the needs of her partners and friends.

Creating rituals or shared activities can also play a significant role in building trust and security. These shared experiences become the threads that weave a stronger, more resilient fabric of connection. For the Type 7, who thrives on new experiences, incorporating variety into these rituals can keep the relationship vibrant and engaging.

Furthermore, setting boundaries is essential. For the enthusiastic woman, boundaries are not limitations but markers of respect and care. They delineate a space where trust can flourish and security can be nurtured, allowing her to freely express her true self within the safety of her relationships.

The Dance of Freedom and Connection

For the Type 7 woman, navigating the dance of freedom and connection in relationships is a journey of continual learning and adaptation. Trust and security are not static destinations but dynamic processes that evolve with each new experience and discovery. By embracing the central role of these elements in her relationships, the

Type 7 woman can cultivate connections that are not only joyful and fulfilling but also deeply rooted in mutual understanding and respect.

In this journey, the ancient wisdom of the Enneagram serves as a guiding light, offering insights that illuminate the path toward building bridges of trust and havens of security. As the Type 7 woman ventures forth, armed with this knowledge, she finds that her relationships become the ultimate adventure—a testament to the beauty of embracing trust, security, and the full spectrum of human connection.

Developing Effective Communication Strategies to Strengthen Bonds with Partners, Friends, and Family

In the mosaic of human relationships, effective communication serves as the mortar that binds individual pieces together, creating a harmonious and resilient structure. For women navigating the journey of personal and relational growth, mastering the art of communication is paramount. This chapter explores how harnessing the ancient wisdom of the Enneagram can empower women to develop communication strategies that not only strengthen bonds with partners, friends, and family but also foster an environment of trust, security, and mutual understanding.

The Foundation of Effective Communication

At its core, effective communication is rooted in authenticity and empathy. It involves the expression of one's thoughts, feelings, and needs in a manner that is clear, respectful, and open to the perspectives of others. For the woman seeking to deepen her connections, the Enneagram offers invaluable insights into the diverse communication styles and needs of each personality type, providing a roadmap for navigating the complex landscape of human interaction.

Tailoring Communication to Personality Types

Understanding the communication preferences and sensitivities of different Enneagram types can significantly enhance interpersonal dynamics. For instance, a Type 2 (The Helper) values expressions of appreciation and recognition, while a Type 5 (The Investigator) may prefer direct, concise communication with plenty of space for processing. By tailoring communication to align with the needs and preferences of each type, women can create a more supportive and nurturing environment for all parties involved.

Strategies for Effective Communication

Active Listening: Beyond merely hearing the words of another, active listening involves fully engaging with the speaker's message, both verbally and nonverbally. This practice fosters a sense of validation and understanding, essential components in building trust and security within relationships.

Expressing Needs and Boundaries Clearly: Utilizing the self-awareness gained through the Enneagram, women can articulate their needs and boundaries more effectively. This clarity prevents misunderstandings and builds a foundation of respect and mutual support.

Navigating Conflict with Compassion: Conflict is an inevitable aspect of any relationship. However, approaching disagreements with a mindset of compassion and a willingness to understand the underlying needs and fears of others can transform conflicts into opportunities for growth and deeper connection.

Cultivating Emotional Intelligence: Emotional intelligence, the ability to recognize, understand, and manage one's own emotions and those of others, is vital for effective communication. The Enneagram aids in developing this intelligence by highlighting the emotional landscapes of each type, enabling women to respond to situations with empathy and insight.

Practicing Vulnerability: True connection is born from vulnerability—the courage to share one's true self, including fears, dreams, and insecurities. By embracing vulnerability in communication, women can foster deeper, more authentic relationships that stand the test of time.

The Path to Joyful Connections

Through the lens of the Enneagram, women are equipped with a powerful tool for enhancing their communication strategies, one that honors the uniqueness of each individual while seeking common ground. By developing skills in active listening, clear expression of needs and boundaries, compassionate conflict resolution, emotional intelligence, and vulnerability, women can strengthen the bonds with their partners, friends, and family, cultivating relationships that are not only joyful but also deeply fulfilling.

In the end, the art of communication is a journey, not a destination. It requires patience, practice, and a willingness to learn and grow. With the Enneagram as a guide, women can navigate this journey with grace and confidence, building bridges of understanding that lead to a life enriched by loving, supportive connections.

Chapter 6:

Igniting Your Spark: Finding Purpose in Career and Vocation

Identifying Your Unique Strengths and Passions to Discover a Fulfilling Career Path

In the journey of self-discovery and personal evolution, the Enneagram serves as a compass, guiding individuals to a deeper understanding of their inner workings and the unique tapestry of traits that define them. For the spirited Type 7 women, this journey entails an exploration into the vibrant realms of their strengths and passions, leading to the illumination of a career path not just walked, but cherished.

Type 7s, known for their enthusiastic, adventurous, and optimistic nature, possess a kaleidoscope of strengths that, when recognized and harnessed, can transform their professional life into an extension of their innermost desires and aspirations. The quest to identify these unique attributes and align them with a fulfilling vocation is akin to igniting a spark within, a spark that lights the way to purposeful engagement and satisfaction in their work.

The initial step in this transformative journey is the acknowledgment of the innate strengths that Type 7s bring to the table. Their adaptability, creativity, and future-oriented vision stand out as beacons of potential in the vast ocean of career possibilities. Type 7s thrive in environments that value innovation, offer variety, and promise personal growth. Recognizing these strengths allows for the exploration of career paths that are not only aligned with their skills but also resonate with their core values and passions.

Passion, the fire that fuels the Type 7's zest for life, is a critical element in the pursuit of a fulfilling career. It is the inner compass that guides them towards vocations that spark joy, excitement, and a profound sense of purpose. The challenge, and indeed the adventure, lies in identifying these passions. Type 7s are encouraged to embark on a journey of self-reflection, exploring past experiences, hobbies, and interests to unearth the themes and activities that bring them the most joy. This introspection is a stepping stone to understanding the deeper motivations behind their passions, providing clarity and direction in the pursuit of a career that fulfills them on all levels.

The synthesis of strengths and passions paves the way for Type 7s to explore career paths that not only cater to their love for excitement and novelty but also offer opportunities for personal and professional growth. Entrepreneurship, creative arts, travel and tourism, and roles that require strategic thinking and problem-solving are just a few avenues where Type 7s can find immense satisfaction and success. The key is to approach this exploration with an open heart and mind, allowing for the possibility that their ideal career may be found in unexpected places.

The journey to finding a fulfilling career path is not without its challenges for Type 7s. Their fear of missing out and tendency to jump from one interest to another may lead to indecision and scattered focus. However, these obstacles also serve as opportunities for growth. By embracing their inner multiplicity and learning to channel their energies into focused pursuits, Type 7 women can navigate their way through the labyrinth of career possibilities to discover their true calling.

Conquering Indecision and Overcoming Fear of Failure in the Workplace

In the odyssey of personal and professional development, Type 7 women encounter unique challenges that stem from their vibrant and exploratory nature. Among these, the twin hurdles of indecision and the fear of failure loom large, casting shadows over their innate potential to thrive and excel in their chosen careers. This segment of their journey calls for a deeper understanding of these challenges, coupled with strategies to transcend them, thereby unlocking the doors to a fulfilling professional life.

The essence of Type 7s—enthusiastic, adventurous, and optimistic—belies an undercurrent of restlessness and a penchant for exploring myriad possibilities. While these qualities are strengths in their own right, they can also give rise to indecision, particularly in the context of career choices and workplace commitments. The vast sea of opportunities available to them can be both exhilarating and overwhelming, leading to a paralysis of choice. This indecision is not merely a matter of choosing between options; it is rooted in a deeper fear of missing out on what each unchosen path might offer.

Moreover, intertwined with indecision is the Type 7's apprehension of failure. Driven by a desire for positive experiences and achievements, the prospect of failing can evoke a sense of vulnerability and inadequacy, steering them away from taking risks or committing to long-term goals. This fear of failure, if left unchecked, can hinder their professional growth and fulfillment, trapping them in a cycle of transient pursuits and unexplored potentials.

To conquer indecision, Type 7 women are encouraged to embrace a process of focused reflection and self-examination. This involves taking a step back to assess their core values, interests, and long-term aspirations.

By grounding their choices in a deeper understanding of what truly matters to them, they can navigate the plethora of options with greater clarity and purpose. Setting smaller, achievable goals along the way can help in building confidence and a sense of direction, gradually alleviating the paralysis that comes with indecision.

Overcoming the fear of failure, on the other hand, requires a shift in perspective. Type 7s can benefit from viewing failure not as a setback but as an integral part of the learning and growth process. Cultivating resilience and a growth mindset empowers them to embrace challenges as opportunities for development, fostering a healthier relationship with risk-taking and commitment. Additionally, seeking out supportive networks and mentors can provide encouragement and guidance, reinforcing their confidence to pursue their aspirations despite potential setbacks.

The journey of Type 7 women in the workplace is one of balance—balancing their enthusiasm for exploration with focused decision-making, and balancing their optimism with the resilience to face and learn from failures. It is through conquering these challenges that they can truly ignite their spark, finding not just success but deep fulfillment in their careers and vocations. The Enneagram, with its rich insights into the human psyche, offers a beacon of light on this journey, guiding Type 7 women towards a path that not only aligns with their strengths and passions but also embraces their vulnerabilities as stepping stones to greatness. In this endeavor, they discover that the true conquest lies not in the absence of fear or indecision but in the courage to move forward, embracing every aspect of their journey with open hearts and minds.

Chapter 7:

Building Inner Strength: Resilience and Self-Acceptance

Developing Resilience to Bounce Back from Challenges and Conquer Self-Criticism

The journey toward self-actualization and inner harmony is a pivotal chapter in the lives of Type 7 women, marked by the pursuit of resilience and self-acceptance. These qualities are not merely aspirational but are foundational in navigating the complexities of life with grace and strength. In this chapter, we delve into the essence of resilience—the capacity to recover from difficulties and the tenacity to face challenges head-on. Coupled with the pivotal role of self-acceptance, these elements forge a path toward profound personal growth and fulfillment.

Resilience, in the context of Type 7 women, is the alchemy of transforming challenges into stepping stones for growth. It is about harnessing their innate enthusiasm and optimism to fuel their journey through adversity. The vibrant spirit of Type 7s, characterized by their desire for exploration and adventure, becomes a crucible for resilience when tempered with the wisdom of experience and self-awareness. Developing resilience involves acknowledging the reality of setbacks and embracing the imperfections of the journey, thereby cultivating a mindset that views challenges as opportunities for learning and evolution.

The process of building resilience is akin to the cultivation of a garden—it requires patience, care, and the acceptance that some days will bring sunshine, while others may bring storms. For Type 7 women, this means actively engaging in self-reflection and mindfulness practices to stay grounded in the present moment, even when their nature tempts them to escape into future possibilities. It involves setting healthy boundaries and learning to say no, which is essential in conserving their energy and focusing on what truly matters. By nurturing their inner resilience, Type 7s can navigate life's ebbs and flows with a sense of purpose and adaptability, ensuring that their zest for life is sustained through all seasons.

Equally vital to the journey of Type 7 women is the embrace of self-acceptance. The shadow of self-criticism often looms over their vibrant personalities, casting doubt on their worthiness and amplifying their fears of inadequacy. Overcoming this inner critic requires a compassionate acknowledgment of their strengths and vulnerabilities. Self-acceptance is the gentle yet powerful recognition that they are enough, just as they are—imperfect, evolving, and whole. It is through this lens of compassion and understanding that Type 7 women can truly appreciate the full spectrum of their being, transforming self-criticism into self-love.

The path to conquering self-criticism lies in the practice of self-compassion, which involves treating oneself with the same kindness and understanding that one would offer to a dear friend. This practice encourages Type 7s to honor their feelings, forgive themselves for their mistakes, and celebrate their successes, no matter how small. It also involves challenging the perfectionist tendencies that can lead to self-doubt, by setting realistic goals and acknowledging the beauty in the journey towards achieving them.

the development of resilience and the journey toward self-acceptance are intertwined paths that lead Type 7 women toward a deeper understanding and appreciation of their true selves. These qualities enable them to bounce back from challenges with grace, to conquer self-criticism with compassion, and to navigate the myriad paths of life with confidence and joy. As they embark on this journey, the teachings of the Enneagram serve as a guide, illuminating the way forward with insights that foster growth, healing, and transformation. Through resilience and self-acceptance, Type 7 women can unlock their full potential, embracing every facet of their vibrant spirit and stepping into a world of limitless possibilities.

Practical Techniques for Managing Anxiety and Cultivating Self-Compassion

In the pursuit of self-discovery and personal growth, Type 7 women face the dual challenges of managing anxiety and cultivating self-compassion. These challenges, while formidable, offer profound opportunities for transformation and empowerment. Drawing from the rich tapestry of the Enneagram's wisdom, this section explores practical techniques designed to guide Type 7 women in navigating these challenges, fostering a deeper sense of peace, self-awareness, and unconditional self-love.

Anxiety, with its myriad forms and manifestations, often acts as a significant barrier to personal fulfillment for Type 7 women. It stems not only from their inherent desire to avoid pain and seek pleasure but also from the deeper fear of being trapped or deprived. To manage anxiety, it is crucial for Type 7s to cultivate mindfulness and grounding techniques that enable them to stay present and connected to their inner experiences without judgment or avoidance.

One effective method for managing anxiety is the practice of mindfulness meditation. By focusing on the breath and observing thoughts and emotions without attachment, Type 7 women can develop a more grounded and centered state of being. This practice helps in acknowledging anxious feelings without being overwhelmed by them, creating space for clarity and calmness. Additionally, incorporating regular mindfulness practices, such as mindful walking or eating, into daily routines can enhance their ability to remain present and reduce the impulse to escape into future planning or fantasies.

Grounding techniques, such as deep breathing exercises, visualization, and sensory engagement, also play a vital role in managing anxiety. For instance, engaging in a brief sensory exercise—focusing on five things you can see, four things you can touch, three things you can hear, two things you can smell, and one thing you can taste—can quickly bring Type 7s back to the present moment, reducing feelings of anxiety and overwhelm.

Cultivating self-compassion is equally essential in the journey of Type 7 women. Self-compassion involves treating oneself with the same kindness, understanding, and support that one would offer to a dear friend. For Type 7s, who may often fall into the trap of self-criticism and perfectionism, learning to extend compassion towards themselves is transformative.

A practical technique for cultivating self-compassion is the practice of self-kindness through affirmations and self-soothing gestures. Repeating affirmations such as "I am worthy of love and kindness" or "I embrace my imperfections with compassion" can reinforce a positive and compassionate self-dialogue. Additionally, physical gestures of comfort, such as placing a hand over the heart or giving oneself a gentle hug, can provide immediate reassurance and foster a sense of self-love.

Journaling is another powerful tool for developing self-compassion. Through reflective writing, Type 7 women can explore their thoughts and emotions in a safe and non-judgmental space. Journaling prompts focused on gratitude, self-forgiveness, and self-appreciation can guide them in recognizing their strengths, acknowledging their efforts, and celebrating their uniqueness.

Chapter 8:

Mind-Body Harmony: Cultivating Wholeness

Exploring the Connection Between Mindful Eating and Your Physical and Emotional Well-being

In the narrative of personal growth and holistic well-being, the journey of Type 7 women encompasses a harmonious integration of mind and body. This chapter delves into the profound practice of mindful eating, a pathway that not only nourishes the body but also enriches the soul, fostering a deep connection between physical sustenance and emotional flourishing.

The concept of mindful eating emerges from the ancient roots of mindfulness, a principle that is deeply interwoven into the fabric of the Enneagram's teachings. It encourages an attentive and intentional relationship with food, one that transcends the mere act of eating to become a mindful practice of awareness, gratitude, and self-care. For Type 7 women, known for their zest for life and a penchant for pleasure, mindful eating offers a transformative approach to experiencing food, one that aligns with their journey towards self-discovery and emotional balance.

Mindful eating is predicated on the awareness of the physical and emotional sensations associated with eating. It invites Type 7 women to slow down, savor each bite, and truly engage with the experience of nourishment. This practice opens the door to recognizing the body's hunger and satiety signals, fostering a healthier relationship with food that is based on need rather than emotional impulses or external stimuli. By embracing mindful eating, Type 7s can explore the intricate connection between their food choices and their physical well-being, leading to more balanced and nutritious eating habits.

Moreover, mindful eating extends beyond the physical aspects of nourishment, touching the realm of emotional well-being. For Type 7 women, the act of eating mindfully can become a moment of reflection, a time to connect with their inner selves and explore the emotional undercurrents that often drive their eating habits. This practice encourages a compassionate inquiry into how emotions such as stress, boredom, or joy influence their relationship with food, offering insights into patterns of emotional eating. Through mindful eating, Type 7s learn to satisfy not just physical hunger but also emotional needs in more constructive and nurturing ways.

The integration of mindful eating into daily life involves practical steps that can lead to profound changes in how Type 7 women relate to food and their bodies. Starting with small, intentional practices such as eating without distractions, taking the time to chew food thoroughly, and expressing gratitude for the meal can significantly enhance the mindful eating experience. These practices encourage a state of presence and appreciation, allowing Type 7s to derive joy and satisfaction from the act of nourishment itself.

In conclusion, the journey towards mind-body harmony for Type 7 women is beautifully supported by the practice of mindful eating. It offers a pathway to cultivating a deeper understanding of their physical and emotional needs, enhancing their well-being through the conscious act of nourishment. As they navigate this journey, the teachings of the Enneagram provide a compass, guiding them towards a holistic integration of mind, body, and spirit. By exploring the connection between mindful eating and their overall well-being, Type 7 women can embrace a more balanced, joyful, and fulfilling way of living, marked by a profound sense of wholeness and self-acceptance.

Discovering the Role of Exercise in Stress Management and Overall Health

In the intricate dance of maintaining equilibrium within the dynamic lives of Type 7 women, the role of exercise emerges as a pivotal element in nurturing both physical and emotional well-being. This chapter explores the multifaceted benefits of physical activity, not just as a tool for maintaining health but as a powerful conduit for stress management, emotional release, and the achievement of a harmonious mind-body balance.

The relationship between exercise and stress relief is well-documented, yet for the Type 7 woman, this connection takes on a deeper significance. Known for their energetic and enthusiastic nature, Type 7s thrive on movement and activity. Exercise, therefore, becomes a natural extension of their zest for life, offering a structured outlet for their boundless energy. Beyond the physical benefits of improved strength, endurance, and health, exercise serves as a meditative practice for Type 7s, allowing them to channel their energy productively, focus their minds, and elevate their spirits.

The impact of exercise on stress management can be attributed to its ability to induce biochemical changes in the brain. Physical activity stimulates the production of endorphins, the body's natural painkillers and mood elevators, often referred to as the "feel-good" hormones. For Type 7 women, the endorphin rush provided by exercise can be particularly therapeutic, offering a natural and healthy escape from stress and anxiety. This biochemical shift not only alleviates stress but also enhances overall emotional well-being, fostering a sense of joy, vitality, and inner peace.

Moreover, exercise plays a crucial role in the regulation of other neurotransmitters, including dopamine, serotonin, and norepinephrine, which are intimately linked to mood and anxiety levels. Regular physical activity helps balance these neurotransmitters, contributing to improved mood stability, reduced anxiety, and a more positive outlook on life. For Type 7 women, who are naturally inclined towards optimism and pleasure, maintaining this biochemical balance through exercise is essential for their emotional health and resilience.

The practice of integrating exercise into daily life requires mindfulness and intentionality, especially for Type 7s, who may be prone to chasing new and exciting experiences. Finding an exercise routine that is enjoyable and stimulating is key to fostering long-term commitment. This might include varied activities that cater to their love of diversity and adventure, such as dance, hiking, yoga, or team sports. The goal is to find a form of exercise that resonates with their personality, encourages consistency, and integrates seamlessly into their lifestyle.

In embracing exercise as a fundamental component of their stress management and health regimen, Type 7 women are invited to explore the deeper connection between physical activity and their emotional landscape. This exploration encourages a holistic approach to well-being, where exercise is not seen merely as a physical endeavor but as a spiritual and emotional practice that nourishes the soul. Through this mindful approach to physical activity, Type 7s can achieve a greater sense of harmony and balance, leading to a fuller, more vibrant life.

the journey towards mind-body harmony for Type 7 women is enriched by the incorporation of exercise into their daily routines. As they discover the profound benefits of physical activity for stress management and overall health, they embark on a path that leads to greater self-awareness, emotional stability, and a deeper connection with their physical selves. Supported by the timeless wisdom of the Enneagram, Type 7 women are empowered to cultivate a holistic sense of well-being that aligns with their dynamic nature, guiding them towards a state of wholeness and fulfillment.

Chapter 9:

Deepening Your Connection: The Enneagram and Spirituality

Utilizing the Enneagram as a Tool to Connect with Your Spiritual Core

In the tapestry of human existence, the search for meaning and connection to something greater than oneself is a universal quest. For Type 7 women, this journey toward spiritual exploration and discovery holds unique significance. It beckons them to dive deeper into their essence, embracing the Enneagram not merely as a map of personality but as a compass guiding them towards their spiritual core. This chapter delves into the sacred intertwining of the Enneagram and spirituality, illuminating pathways for Type 7 women to foster a profound connection with their innermost being.

The Enneagram, with its ancient roots and mystical origins, serves as a bridge between the temporal and the eternal, the personal and the universal. Its framework offers more than insights into personality traits; it presents a transformative journey of self-awareness, healing, and growth. For Type 7 women, known for their joyous spirit and enthusiasm for life, the Enneagram provides a reflective mirror, revealing deeper truths about their desires, fears, and motivations. It invites them to explore the spiritual dimensions of their being, encouraging a journey inward to discover the wellspring of joy, peace, and fulfillment that resides within.

Utilizing the Enneagram as a spiritual tool involves engaging with it on a profound level, beyond the identification with one's type. It encompasses a process of introspection and self-inquiry, where Type 7 women are called to examine their inner landscapes, confront their shadows, and embrace their light. This process encourages them to question, reflect, and meditate on their life's purpose, their relationships, and their connection to the divine.

One practical approach to deepening this spiritual connection is through contemplative practices aligned with the Enneagram's wisdom. Meditation, prayer, and journaling can become sacred rituals that help Type 7s attune to their inner voice and the whispers of their soul. These practices can be tailored to reflect the dynamic nature of Type 7 women, incorporating movement, music, or art as mediums for spiritual expression and exploration.

Moreover, the Enneagram's teachings on the virtues and holy ideas associated with each type serve as spiritual guideposts. For Type 7s, the virtue of Sobriety and the holy idea of Holy Work or Holy Plan offer profound insights into embracing the present moment, finding satisfaction in the here and now, and aligning with a higher purpose. By reflecting on these concepts, Type 7 women can cultivate a sense of inner balance and harmony, learning to navigate life's ups and downs with grace and equanimity.

The journey towards connecting with one's spiritual core is also a path of healing and transformation. It requires facing one's fears, embracing vulnerability, and letting go of attachments that no longer serve. For Type 7 women, this might mean confronting the fear of pain or deprivation and learning to trust in the process of life. Through the Enneagram's guidance, they can learn to welcome all aspects of their experience, finding beauty and wisdom in both joy and sorrow.

the Enneagram offers Type 7 women a profound tool for spiritual exploration and growth, inviting them to embark on a journey of self-discovery that leads to their spiritual core. By engaging with the Enneagram's wisdom, embracing contemplative practices, and reflecting on the virtues and holy ideas, Type 7 women can deepen their connection to themselves and the divine. This journey is not a destination but a continuous unfolding, a path of becoming that reveals the luminous essence of their being. Through this sacred exploration, Type 7 women can discover a wellspring of spiritual depth, enriching their lives with meaning, purpose, and a profound sense of connection to all that is.

Exploring Various Spiritual Practices That Resonate with the Type 7 Woman

In the rich landscape of spiritual exploration, the Type 7 woman stands at the crossroads of curiosity and desire for depth, seeking practices that not only resonate with her vibrant spirit but also anchor her in a profound sense of connection and purpose. This chapter ventures into the realm of spiritual practices tailored to the essence of Type 7 women, embracing the diversity of paths that align with their joyful pursuit of growth and fulfillment.

For the Type 7 woman, spirituality is not confined to traditional or orthodox methods; it is a living, breathing journey that celebrates freedom, exploration, and the joy of discovery. Recognizing this, we delve into a selection of spiritual practices that mirror the dynamic nature of Type 7s, offering them avenues to deepen their spiritual connection in ways that are authentic, engaging, and transformative.

Mindfulness and Meditation: While meditation is a cornerstone practice for many spiritual traditions, Type 7 women might find dynamic forms of meditation particularly enriching. Practices such as walking meditation, dance meditation, or even mindfulness during exercise can be powerful ways for Type 7s to connect with the present moment, harness their energy, and find peace in the here and now. These forms of meditation embrace movement and change, resonating with the Type 7's love for activity and variety.

Nature Connection: The natural world offers a profound source of spiritual nourishment for Type 7 women. Activities such as hiking, gardening, or simply spending time in contemplation outdoors can facilitate a deep connection to the earth and the cycles of life. These experiences can help Type 7s feel grounded and remind them of the interconnectedness of all things, fostering a sense of harmony and belonging.

Creative Expression: Artistic endeavors such as painting, writing, music, or crafts can serve as meditative practices that connect Type 7 women to their inner worlds and the divine creativity that flows through them. Engaging in creative expression allows them to explore their emotions, thoughts, and spiritual insights in a tangible form, providing both a source of joy and a tool for reflection and growth.

Volunteering and Service: Given their enthusiastic and optimistic nature, Type 7 women may find deep spiritual fulfillment in acts of service and volunteering. Engaging in work that helps others and contributes to a greater good can provide a sense of purpose and connection, aligning with the Type 7's desire to make a positive impact in the world. This practice also offers a way to step outside oneself, fostering empathy, gratitude, and a broader perspective on life.

Exploration of Wisdom Traditions: Type 7 women, with their natural curiosity and love for learning, may be drawn to the exploration of various spiritual and wisdom traditions. Studying the teachings of different cultures and philosophies can provide a rich tapestry of insights and practices to integrate into their own spiritual journey. This exploration allows Type 7s to weave together a personalized spiritual path that resonates with their unique perspectives and experiences.

Retreats and Workshops: Participating in spiritual retreats or workshops offers Type 7 women the opportunity to immerse themselves in intensive spiritual practice, surrounded by a community of like-minded individuals. These experiences can be particularly transformative, providing dedicated time and space for introspection, learning, and growth. Retreats focused on themes such as silence, meditation, yoga, or specific spiritual teachings can cater to the Type 7's desire for adventure and profound connection.

the spiritual journey for Type 7 women is an invitation to explore, discover, and connect with the depth of their being in ways that reflect their dynamic essence. By engaging with spiritual practices that resonate with their innate joy, curiosity, and desire for growth, Type 7 women can cultivate a rich, fulfilling spiritual life. Through this exploration, they deepen their connection to themselves, the divine, and the world around them, embarking on a path of discovery that is both exhilarating and deeply rewarding.

Chapter 10:

Unveiling Your Wings: Exploring the Nuances of Your Personality

Delving into the Concept of Wings (Type 7w6 and Type 7w8) and Their Influence on Your Strengths, Challenges, and Overall Personality

In the intricate journey of self-discovery through the Enneagram, understanding one's dominant type provides profound insights into their core motivations, fears, and behaviors. However, the exploration does not end there. For Type 7 women, delving deeper into the nuances of their personality involves examining the concept of wings—adjacent types that exert a significant influence on their primary type, enhancing the complexity and richness of their character. This chapter focuses on the wings of Type 7: Type 6 (The Loyalist) and Type 8 (The Challenger), and how these influences sculpt their strengths, challenges, and the tapestry of their personality.

Type 7w6: The Entertaining Optimist

Type 7 women with a 6 wing (7w6) blend the enthusiasm and exploratory zest of Type 7 with the responsibility and loyalty of Type 6. This combination creates a personality that is both playful and committed, innovative and cautious. The 7w6s are characterized by their engaging charm, wit, and a more pronounced sense of loyalty and warmth towards their friends and causes they believe in. Their Six wing introduces a layer of anxiety and skepticism, which tempers the Seven's natural inclination toward optimism and impulsivity.

The 7w6's strengths lie in their ability to be both visionary and practical. They excel in environments where they can innovate while being part of a team or community. Their blend of foresight and dedication makes them excellent collaborators who can inspire and motivate others with their ideas and enthusiasm, while also being attuned to potential risks and outcomes.

However, the inclusion of the Six wing also brings challenges. The 7w6 may find themselves torn between their desire for new experiences and a simultaneous fear of stepping too far out of their comfort zone. This internal conflict can lead to indecision or anxiety, particularly in situations requiring commitment or when facing the unknown.

Type 7w8: The Assertive Adventurer

On the other side, Type 7 women with an 8 wing (7w8) embody the joyfulness and spontaneity of Type 7, infused with the assertiveness and decisiveness of Type 8. These individuals are dynamic, direct, and possess an innate confidence in pursuing their desires. The 7w8s are known for their assertiveness, energy, and willingness to take the lead in adventures or entrepreneurial ventures. Their Eight wing adds a layer of strength and protectiveness, making them formidable advocates for themselves and others.

Strengths of the 7w8 include their exceptional ability to confront challenges head-on, combined with the creativity and optimism to envision positive outcomes. They thrive in situations where they can be autonomous, lead initiatives, or when their passion can drive them to inspire and rally others toward a common goal.

The challenges for 7w8s stem from their intense desire for independence and experience, which can sometimes overshadow the need for introspection and emotional depth. Their Eight wing's intensity and assertiveness may also lead to conflicts, especially if their approach is perceived as too forceful or their desire for excitement overrides caution.

Integrating the Wings into the Whole

For Type 7 women, recognizing and integrating their wing influences is a journey of balancing the vibrant energy and optimism of the Seven with the loyalty and analytical prowess of the Six or the assertiveness and strength of the Eight. This exploration enables them to harness a broader spectrum of strengths while addressing the challenges that arise from the interplay of these dynamic forces.

Embracing the full scope of their personality, including the nuances introduced by their wings, allows Type 7 women to navigate life with a richer understanding of themselves and their interactions with the world. It offers a pathway to growth that honors their complexity, enabling them to live with authenticity, resilience, and a deepened capacity for joy and connection.

the wings of the Enneagram Type 7—the 6 and the 8—serve not only to enhance the understanding of their primary type but also to illuminate the diverse pathways of development and self-realization available to them. By delving into these influences, Type 7 women can unlock new dimensions of their personality, fostering a holistic approach to their growth and evolution. The journey through the nuances of their character is an invitation to embrace the fullness of their being, unveiling their wings to soar into a life of depth, purpose, and boundless potential.

Chapter 11:

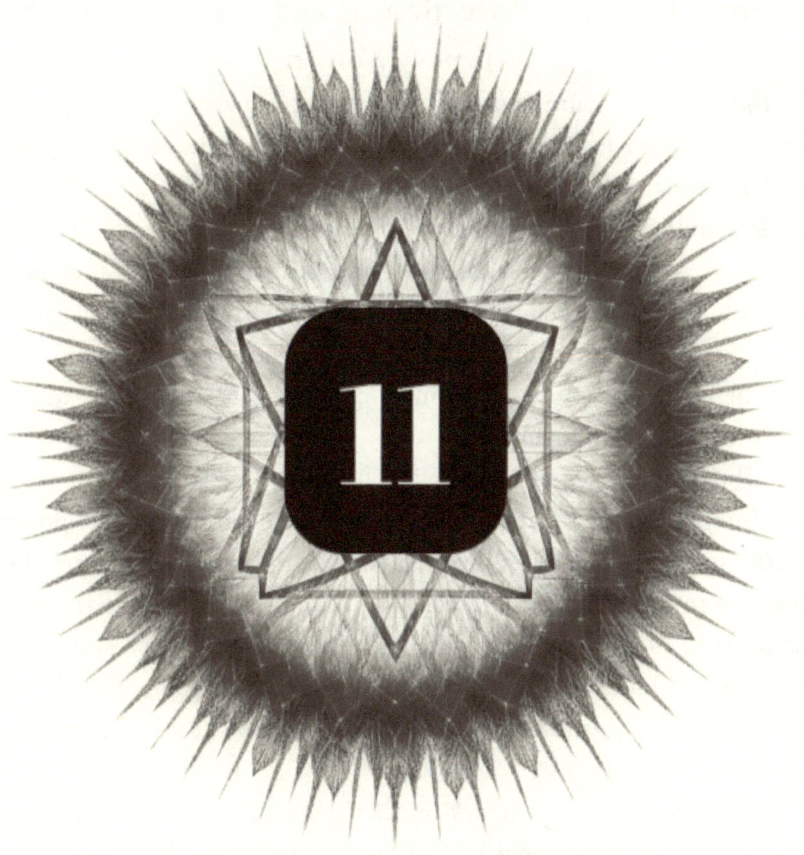

Growth and Transformation: Integration and Disintegration

Understanding the Path of Integration Towards Type 5 (Increased Focus and Discipline) and Disintegration Towards Type 1 (Perfectionism and Negativity) for the Type 7 Woman

In the enriching journey of self-awareness and personal evolution that the Enneagram facilitates, each type faces its unique path of growth and potential pitfalls. For the Type 7 woman, this journey involves understanding the dynamics of integration towards Type 5, characterized by an increased focus and discipline, and disintegration towards Type 1, marked by a shift towards perfectionism and negativity. This chapter aims to illuminate these transformative paths, offering insight into how Type 7 women can navigate their way towards wholeness and fulfillment.

The Path of Integration: Moving Towards Type 5

Integration for a Type 7 involves a movement towards the positive attributes of Type 5 – The Investigator. This shift represents a profound journey towards embracing depth, focus, and discipline. In their core state, Type 7s are known for their enthusiasm, spontaneity, and a desire for variety. However, this boundless energy can sometimes lead to scattered focus, restlessness, and an avoidance of deeper emotional or complex issues.

As Type 7 women embark on their path of integration, they begin to incorporate the strengths of Type 5, harnessing their energy with a newfound focus and becoming more comfortable with solitude and introspection. This does not mean that they lose their zest for life or their curiosity. Instead, they learn to channel these traits into more focused and sustained endeavors, allowing for a deeper exploration of subjects and interests. They become more adept at observing their impulses without immediately acting on them, cultivating a space of inner calm and clarity.

This integration process enables Type 7 women to engage more fully with their inner world and the world around them, embracing complexity and uncertainty with patience and curiosity. Their minds become enriched with a depth of knowledge and insight, enhancing their creative and intellectual pursuits. Discipline, once perceived as a limitation, becomes a tool for freedom, allowing them to delve deeper into their passions and achieve their goals with determination and resilience.

The Path of Disintegration: Moving Towards Type 1

Disintegration for a Type 7 involves moving in the direction of the less healthy attributes of Type 1 – The Reformer. This shift is characterized by an emerging perfectionism and an inclination towards negativity, particularly under stress or when their desires for freedom and happiness are thwarted. Type 7s, in their pursuit of joy and avoidance of pain, may find themselves fixating on idealistic standards or becoming overly critical of themselves and others when reality falls short of their expectations.

The challenge for Type 7 women on this path is to recognize the early signs of disintegration and understand that their critical nature or perfectionism is often a defense mechanism against facing deeper fears and disappointments. It reflects a struggle to maintain control and avoid negative emotions, but it can lead to a rigid and judgmental attitude that stifles their natural openness and joy.

Embracing the lessons of Type 1 can be transformative if approached with awareness and compassion. It involves acknowledging the value of structure and discipline not as constraints but as supports for their growth and happiness. Learning to accept imperfection – both in themselves and in the world around them – can open the door to a more authentic and compassionate way of being. It allows them to see the beauty in the process, rather than being solely focused on the outcome, and to cultivate patience and understanding in their journey towards fulfillment.

Navigating the Journey

The journey of integration and disintegration for the Type 7 woman is a dynamic process of self-discovery and transformation. It invites a deeper engagement with their strengths and vulnerabilities, encouraging a balance between their desire for freedom and joy and the embrace of focus, depth, and discipline. By recognizing the potential for growth in the attributes of both Type 5 and the lessons to be learned from the challenges of moving towards Type 1, Type 7 women can navigate their path with wisdom and grace. This journey, though fraught with challenges, holds the promise of leading them to a richer, more fulfilling experience of life, where the vibrancy of their personality is not diminished but deepened, unveiling the true breadth of their wings.

Chapter 12:

Workbook

Did you love *The woman of Enneagram 7: Love marriage success edition*? Then you should read *The Woman of Enneagram 6: Love, Marriage, Success Edition*[1] by Maria Rondon!

Discover the life-changing power of the Enneagram as a Type 6 woman. This invaluable book provides profound insights into the core motivations, strengths, and growth opportunities for the Loyal Skeptic personality type.

As an Enneagram Type 6, you possess a deep commitment to truth, security, and belonging. However, these qualities can sometimes manifest as anxiety, doubt, and a tendency to play devil's advocate. This book empowers you to embrace your essence while breaking free from limiting fears and reactivity.

---

1. https://books2read.com/u/bWoKj0

2. https://books2read.com/u/bWoKj0

Through thought-provoking exercises and relatable examples, you'll explore how the Enneagram impacts your relationships, career, and personal growth journey. Gain a deeper understanding of your need for safety and support systems. Learn to cultivate courage in the face of uncertainty and develop self-assured confidence.

Whether seeking to improve intimacy, find career fulfillment, or live with greater inner peace, this book is a powerful ally. It offers practical strategies to help you harness the strengths of Type 6 - loyalty, responsibility, and foresight - while addressing core fears of abandonment and instability.

Dive into this transformative read and embark on a journey of profound self-discovery and personal empowerment. Unlock your true potential as an Enneagram Type 6 woman. Live with greater trust, resilience, and alignment with your authentic self.

Also by Maria Rondon

Alzheimer
Alzheimer Guia para cuidadores

Enneagram For Women
The woman of Enneagram 1: Love Marriage Success Edition
The woman of enneagram 2
The woman of Enneagram 3: Love marriage success edition
The Woman of Enneagram 4: Love, Marriage, Success Edition
The woman of Enneagram 5: Love marriage success edition
The Woman of Enneagram 6: Love, Marriage, Success Edition
The woman of Enneagram 7: Love marriage success edition
The woman of Enneagram 8: Love marriage success edition
The woman of Enneagram 9: Love marriage success edition

LOA
El secreto para atraer tu alma gemela

Standalone

Keto Low-Carb Mexican Cookbook
Plant Powered Cookbook: The Ultimate Vegan Cookbook for Healthy Living
The Destiny Matrix